W9-DJQ-004

DRUGS ON YOUR STREETS

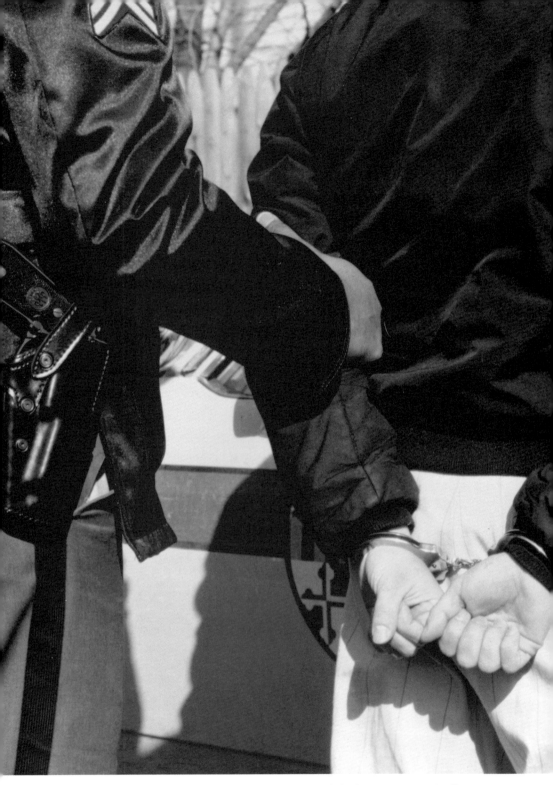

Trying drugs can lead to a downhill slide from using to dealing to arrest and jail.

DRUGS ON YOUR STREETS

Gabrielle Edwards

THE ROSEN PUBLISHING GROUP, INC.
NEW YORK

The people in this book are only models; they in no way practice or endorse the the activities illustrated. Captions serve only to explain the subjects of the photographs and do not imply a connection between real-life models and the staged situations shown. News agency photographs are exceptions.

Published in 1991,1994, 1998 by The Rosen Publishing Group, Inc.
29 East 21st Street, New York, NY 10010

Revised Edition 1998

Copyright © 1991,1994, 1998 by The Rosen Publishing Group, Inc.

Library of Congress Cataloging-in-Publication Data

Edwards, Gabrielle.
    Drugs on your streets / Gabrielle Edwards.
    (The Drug abuse prevention library)
    Includes bibliographical references and index.
    Summary: Discusses various drugs and their dangers and presents survival techniques for existing in a drug-infested neighborhood.
    ISBN 0-8239-2615-X
    1. Drug abuse—Juvenile literature. 2. Drug abuse—United States—Juvenile literature. 3. Drugs—Physiological effect—Juvenile literature. [1. Drugs. 2. Drug abuse.] I. Title. II. Series.
HV5809.5.E38 1991
362.29—dc20   91-18369
                                                  CIP
                                                      AC

Manufactured in the United States of America

Contents

Introduction

*R*osalee liked the look of the models in the magazines. They were all so thin, and their skin was so pale. Her friends told her that they looked like that because they smoked heroin. Rosalee was convinced that boys would find her more attractive if she looked like those models. So she bought some heroin from a guy in one of her classes. "Heroin is going to help me to look better," thought Rosalee as she breathed deeply from the plastic pipe in her hand.

Trevor was in the eighth grade. Most of his friends smoked marijuana. Trevor started smoking it a few months ago—he didn't think it was a big deal. At the last party, a friend offered him some crack. Trevor tried it and loved the intense high it gave him. Soon he was hooked.

A drug is a substance that changes the way your body works. Not all drugs are bad. In fact—many drugs, called medicines, help sick people feel better. These drugs are legal, and many require a prescription from a doctor. Other legal drugs, such as caffeine, are available to everyone. Alcohol and tobacco are also drugs, and they are legal to people over a certain age. There are also illegal drugs. These drugs, such as heroin, cocaine, and marijuana, are considered dangerous and addictive, and they are the focus of this book. The abuse of illegal drugs has become an enormous problem in many countries, especially the United States. The streets have become a haven for drug users and dealers.

In this book you will learn about the many different kinds of drugs being sold on the streets today and what those drugs can do to your body and mind. You will learn why people try drugs and some of the reasons they become addicted. You will also read about ways to find help if drugs have become part of your life. You will read about choices that some young people have made about drugs. The goal is to provide you with enough information to help you make your own choices about staying away from drugs and keeping safe and healthy.

Drugs affect all the workings of the body—even the ability to make an easy pool shot.

CHAPTER 1

What Are Street Drugs?

*L*ela *was a little nervous about walking home by herself so late in the evening, but rehearsals for the school play took longer than usual. Lela's mom had to work late and couldn't pick her up. Lela didn't like her neighborhood very much. She knew people were dealing drugs, especially when it got dark.*

Suddenly a man came up her. "Hey, sweetie, want to have some fun?" He pulled a small bag of white powder from his pocket and waved it in front of her.

"No, thank you," replied Lela. She began to walk faster.

"Come on, you'll enjoy it. No charge," the man said as he walked faster to keep up with her.

"No!" shouted Lela, and she started running.

10

Luckily, the man didn't follow her. Lela's heart was pounding. It wasn't fair that she couldn't feel safe walking in her own neighborhood. Why couldn't the police or somebody clean up the streets and stop these drug dealers?

You may live in a neighborhood like Lela's or you may have had someone offer you drugs. It can be a frightening experience, especially if you know how dangerous drugs can be. However, you may also be tempted to try a drug at some point. You should be aware of the dangers of street drugs: They can be deadly.

A street drug is any drug bought on the street for the purpose of getting high. Any drug sold on the streets is illegal, even if it has medicinal value. Prescription drugs, such as Ritalin or Valium, must be prescribed by doctors and are meant to be used by people with medical problems, and they are also sold on the streets. These drugs are illegal when they are bought without a prescription from a doctor.

The most commonly abused street drugs are illegal drugs, such as heroin and crack. Approximately 12 million people in the United States use illegal drugs. According to an article in the May 1997 issue of *Time* magazine, 200,000 people used heroin in

Cocaine has become a major killer on American highways.

the past month, 800,000 used amphetamines, 1.5 million used cocaine/crack, and
more than 10 million people used marijuana.

Street drugs are made from different
ingredients. Some drugs are called natural
drugs because they are derived from plants.
These include heroin, cocaine, and marijuana. Other drugs, called synthetic drugs,
are made from chemicals. These drugs
include PCP, China White, and Ecstasy.

Street drugs can affect the body in different ways. They can have both physical and
psychological effects. Some of the drugs give
users a high, a feeling of extreme excitement
or happiness. The drugs' effects, the high,
and how long the high lasts all depend on the
drug and how much of the drug is used. *11*

Drug users may become paranoid—afraid of their own shadow.

Stimulants

Some drugs speed up your bodily functions, including heartbeat, breathing, movements, and speech. These kinds of drugs are called stimulants. They include cocaine, crack, and amphetamines. They often create a short, intense high. After the drug wears off, the user "crashes." He or she may feel extremely tired and drained and may sleep for twenty-four hours or longer.

Narcotics

Narcotics are part of a larger group of drugs called downers because these drugs tend to depress or slow down the functions of the body. Narcotics, also called opiates, are made from the seeds of a type of poppy plant. Some narcotics, such as morphine, have medical uses. They are used to control pain, especially during or after surgery. Heroin, on the other hand, is a widely abused illegal narcotic sold on the streets.

Hallucinogens

Hallucinogens distort reality and cause the user to hallucinate—to see or hear things that aren't there. Users may also see and hear things in a distorted way. Hallucinogens include marijuana, LSD (lysergic acid diethy-

14 lamide), PCP (phencyclidine), peyote, and magic mushrooms.

Tranquilizers

Tranquilizers are the final group of street drugs that we will discuss in this book. Tranquilizers are used to reduce anxiety or to relax someone. These drugs include Valium and Rohypnol. Users on tranquilizers often appear drunk. They may stagger and slur their words, or even fall asleep.

These groups of drugs will be discussed in greater detail later in this book.

CHAPTER 2

The Dangers of Experimenting

*A*nthony was nervous and excited on the morning of his first day at high school. High school is completely different than junior high. He hoped he would fit in. Near the end of the day, Veronica, a girl on the cheerleading squad, asked Anthony to come to a party at her house on Friday. Anthony was so excited. He was going to hang out with the "cool" people in school.

When Anthony showed up at Veronica's house, he knew this party would be unlike any other party he had been to. People were drinking beer and smoking. Veronica welcomed him by offering him a beer. Anthony had tried beer before. He really didn't like the taste of it, but he didn't want to seem like a geek so he took the can.

After a couple of beers, Anthony was feeling light-headed. Veronica took his hand and led

15

Many teens experiment with drugs because of peer pressure, boredom, or as a way to escape from problems.

him into the bathroom. She pulled out a joint *from her pocket and lit it. She took a couple of puffs and then offered it to Anthony.*

"Come on," Veronica said, "let's have some real fun." Anthony wasn't thinking too clearly because of the beer, but he figured that it couldn't hurt. He really liked Veronica and wanted her to like him too so he took a drag of the joint.

Not long after that, Anthony was a regular at the parties. He was willing to try anything that was offered to him.

Using drugs is a dangerous and expensive habit, and it is a habit often formed during the teenage years. During this time, teens make the sometimes difficult transition from children to adults. They face anxieties from their changing bodies, and pressure from friends and families. It is also during this time that teens may begin to learn more about the world and question what they were taught as children.

Why Do Teens Experiment?

Many teens who experiment with drugs are curious or bored. Some hope that using drugs will help them fit in. Others believe that using drugs will make them seem more grown-up or self-confident.

18 Some teens hope drugs will make their problems go away. In order to deal with the pressure that some teens face in school and at home, they may turn to drugs to provide an escape or another reality.

One of the most common reasons teens choose to experiment with drugs is peer pressure. At a party, you may see friends lighting up marijuana joints. You may think it's no big deal to take a puff, since everyone else is doing it. Or you may go along with it so people don't think you're weird or scared.

Increasing Numbers of Teens Experimenting

According to the National Household Survey on Drug Abuse, drug use among teenagers has almost doubled since 1992. Some people credit this increase to the casual attitude that some teens have towards drugs and the increasing pressure from other teens to experiment with drugs.

What many of these experimenting teens are unaware of is the danger presented by drug use. Most of them don't think drugs will harm them or that they could become addicted to the drugs.

Drugs and Addiction

Addiction is a disease in which an addict loses control over his or her use of a drug. People who become addicted to drugs often cannot quit using drugs without help.

Addiction is a complicated matter. Why and how do people become addicted? Why do some people become addicted and others do not? To answer these questions, we need to focus on the main part of the body affected by drugs—the brain.

When a drug enters the body, it upsets the normal chemical balance. It affects the parts of the brain that control breathing, eating, and sleeping. With this balance upset, people high on drugs may lose their inhibitions and behave differently or do things they normally would not do. Drugs also affect their moods and their coordination. Every drug affects the body differently, but the one thing that most drugs have in common is that they elevate the levels of a chemical in the brain called dopamine.

Dopamine and Addiction

Recently scientists have discovered what they believe may be a link between dopamine and drug addiction. Dopamine is the chemical that allows you to feel plea-

20 | sure and elation. A hug, a kiss, or a feeling of accomplishment can all raise the level of dopamine in the body, thereby making a person feel happy and excited. But many drugs, such as cocaine, also increase the dopamine level. Because the increased level of dopamine makes users feel good, many will take a drug again and again to repeat the good feeling. With each use, the brain begins to depend on the drug more and more to reach the levels of pleasure it once attained from a hug, a kiss, or a feeling of accomplishment.

Physical Addiction

Once a person's brain begins to rely on a drug to feel normal, that person has become physically addicted to the drug. The use of drugs upsets the balance of chemicals in the brain. The brain begins to produce greater or lesser amounts of its chemicals to compensate for the chemicals found in the drugs. Eventually the brain needs the chemicals from the drugs to reach the correct balance. Without the drugs, the brain does not function properly.

The person's body will also develop tolerance to a drug. This means that a higher dosage of the drug is needed to keep the brain and body functioning properly.

Some people mistakenly believe they can escape their problems with drugs, but their problems will still be there when their high wears off.

Psychological Addiction

As mentioned earlier, people take drugs for many different reasons. Some people take drugs to escape their problems. Others take drugs because they believe the drug gives them more confidence or more energy. When a person begins to rely on a drug to cope with problems or to gain more confidence, he or she has become psychologically addicted to the drug.

Many addicts don't realize that drugs aren't the answer to their problems. Whatever problems they had will still be there when they come down from their high.

22 | *Why Do Some People Become Addicted?*

Another relatively recent scientific discovery points to the likelihood that some people are more prone to become addicted than others. A person's genetic makeup determines his or her looks, personality, behavior, and chemical balance in the brain. It is this balance that determines how the brain will respond to drugs, and the rate at which the brain can "reset" itself to the correct chemical balance after drugs are taken. For example, if a person's body doesn't produce enough dopamine, his or her brain may become more easily addicted to the drugs that increase dopamine production. If you have a family member, such as a parent, uncle, aunt or grandparent, who is addicted to drugs, you may have a greater chance of becoming addicted to drugs. Nearly 95 percent of cocaine users are children of addicted parents.

CHAPTER 3

Drugs in Your Neighborhood

*I*t was Beau's turn to baby-sit his little sister, Emme. It was a beautiful day, and he decided to take her to the playground. Emme was playing in the sandbox with a few other children when she found something in the sand and began playing with it. Beau took it from Emme. It was a crack pipe.

Beau exploded and started yelling at Emme never to play with things she finds on the ground. Emme began to cry. Beau looked at his sister and realized he wasn't angry at Emme—he was mad at the drug users who left the pipe behind. He was frightened that Emme might have hurt herself on the pipe. A few years earlier, this would have never happened. Their neighborhood used to be safe and free of drugs

23

Drugs in a neighborhood make everyone feel nervous and threatened.

and crime. Now it wasn't even safe to let his
sister play at the playground. Beau apologized
to Emme, and he took her home. He realized
there may be no safe place on the street for his
sister to play.

Until recently, drug neighborhoods were usually found in big cities, such as New York City or Los Angeles. However, in the past few years drugs have begun infiltrating even small, rural towns in the Midwest. Drug use is a growing problem that affects many neighborhoods and communities across the country.

When drugs become a part of a neighborhood, they can drastically change it. Along with the drugs come drug dealers, crime, and violence. Drugs are a big business involving billions of dollars. With this much money involved, people in the business will do whatever it takes to protect their products.

Drugs and Gangs

Gangs play an important role in the drug world and the neighborhoods it rules. Once drugs hit the streets, gang members are often the people who sell them. The gangs can be small, loosely organized, or large and sophisticated.

Each gang tends to control the drugs in a certain neighborhood or territory. However, rival gangs may try to take control of a certain territory. When this happens, violence is usually the result. Innocent people are often caught in the crossfire of gang wars or are hit by stray bullets during vengeful drive-by shootings.

Drugs and Violence

Gangs use an organized business-like approach to create new markets for their drugs. They approach a neighborhood and pass out free samples. Those who try the drugs will most likely come back for more. However, this time the drugs are not free. Before long, a market is created.

Gangs may also recruit addicts to work for them. These jobs may include delivering drugs, acting as a look-out while a deal takes place, or directing customers to where they can buy drugs. Some young users are given drugs and told to pass out free samples in their schools or to their friends in order to build a younger market.

Most users who become addicted will do anything to get more drugs. Dealers know this, and they often introduce addicts to crimes, such as robbery, burglary, and prostitution. Dealers then trade drugs for stolen goods.

Gangs aren't the only ones who bring violence to neighborhoods infested with drugs. Drug users also commit crimes and acts of violence in their communities while they are high. Drug addicts often steal from family, friends, rob strangers, and burglarize homes and stores.

Prostitution

Some drug addicts are willing to become prostitutes—have sex for money—to buy drugs. Some walk the streets, waiting for someone to pick them up and trade sex for money. Then they buy drugs with this money. Other addicts may trade sex with the dealer for drugs. Sometimes a dealer sells the use of a drug addict's body to someone else. The addicts usually don't care what happens as long as they get more drugs.

Drug-addicted prostitutes face many dangers because they care so little about anything other than getting more drugs. Most do not think about birth control or safe sex when they engage in sexual activities. The result is that many risk contracting sexually transmitted diseases, such as AIDS, or becoming pregnant.

CHAPTER 4

Hallucinogens

*H*allucinogens are drugs that change a person's perception of reality. Hallucinogens cause users to hallucinate, which means they see and hear things that are not real or see or hear real things in a distorted way.

Drugs in this category include marijuana, LSD, phencyclidine (PCP), mescaline, peyote, and magic mushrooms.

Marijuana

Marijuana, also known as "pot," "grass," or "weed," is one of the most commonly abused drugs in the United States. It is illegal to use marijuana except in two states, California and Arizona, which

Marijuana may cause some users to lose interest in school, friends, and family.

recently passed laws allowing for medical use of marijuana. Marijuana is usually smoked in hand-rolled cigarettes called joints.

Marijuana is made from the cannabis, or hemp, plant. This plant contains over 400 chemicals, but the ingredient that causes hallucinations is Tetrahydrocannabinal, or THC.

Marijuana affects both the body and the mind. When someone smokes marijuana, he or she tries to hold in the smoke for as long as possible. This is dangerous for the lungs. Long-term effects may include lung cancer and lung disease.

The brain is also affected by marijuana.

30 The effects of marijuana are felt about fifteen to twenty minutes after it is smoked. The user may feel relaxed, drowsy, or happy. He or she may have hallucinations for several hours. He or she may have trouble remembering things from one minute to the next. Marijuana affects the brain's short-term memory functions. Over time memory may be permanently affected.

According to a study conducted by Dr. Walter Lehman, many teenagers who use marijuana show a decline in personal habits. Users stop caring about such things as school, family, and even their appearance. Studies also show marijuana is often the first drug with which many teens experiment. For this reason, marijuana is known as a gateway drug because many users gradually go on to use harder drugs.

Ecstasy

Ecstasy, sometimes called "X," or "E," is a synthetic drug. Officially it is classified as a hallucinogen because it causes users to see things in distorted ways. But its effects are similar to that of amphetamines, which means it speeds up the functions of the body.

Ecstasy has recently grown in popularity due to parties called raves. Raves are held in abandoned warehouses, parks, or nightclubs. Many people who go to raves get high on Ecstasy, which enables them to dance all night. The music, the crowd of dancers, and the spinning lights add intensity to the high.

While Ecstasy can give an intense high, it can also cause bad trips. Some people feel panic, confusion, paranoia, or even suffer from a panic attack when on the drug. When the drug wears off, the user may experience body chills, muscle or joint pains, and irritability. Some users also become depressed and very tired.

Ecstasy comes in different forms: tablet, capsule, or powder. Although it is usually taken orally, it can also be snorted, injected, or smoked.

LSD

LSD, also known as acid, is a synthetic drug, which means it is made in a laboratory. LSD is made from the fungus that grows on rye and other grains. LSD is a colorless, odorless, and tasteless white powder. It can be made into tablets, capsules, or a liquid.

LSD changes the way the brain works. Users feel the effects of LSD thirty to ninety minutes after taking it. The effects can last up to twelve hours. LSD causes hallucinations known as "trips." There is no way to

32 predict whether it will be a good or bad trip.

The physical effects of LSD include sweating, sleeplessness, a dry mouth, loss of appetite, and the shakes. A person's heart rate, body temperature, and blood pressure may increase. LSD can cause a user to feel panic, confusion, anxiety, or a loss of control.

LSD is such a powerful drug that it never completely leaves the body. Even if someone has only used LSD once, he or she can experience an LSD flashback days, weeks, or even years later.

PCP

Also known as "angel dust," PCP is another synthetic drug. PCP comes in powder, liquid, pill, or capsule form. It can be swallowed in tablet or capsule form, or be sniffed or injected.

PCP was first used by veterinarians to sedate large animals. However, it disturbed the animals so much before putting them to sleep that its use was stopped.

Taken in small doses by humans, PCP increases blood pressure, body temperature, heart rate, and sweating. The effects of the drugs are unpredictable. PCP may induce users to a state of euphoria or panic and loss of control. Users can turn violent or behave

Ordinary things can look strange and terrifying to a person on an LSD trip.

strangely. PCP can also lead to heart failure, lung failure, or even stroke. Sometimes the effects of PCP can make users seem like they are suffering from schizophrenia.

Mescaline and Peyote

Peyote is a short, spineless cactus plant. The top of the cactus has a little button which contains a chemical called mescaline. The mind-changing abilities of mescaline have been known for hundreds of years. The Aztecs of South America used peyote in religious ceremonies. Some Native American

33

34 tribes continue to use peyote in some of their religious ceremonies.

Peyote can be eaten fresh or dried. If dried it can then be eaten whole or used to make tea. Mescaline can also be synthetically produced.

Mescaline causes hallucinations. The user will see or hear things that aren't really there. The hallucinations can be frightening and can last for ten to twelve hours. Users often experience nausea and vomiting.

Magic Mushrooms

Magic mushrooms contain a chemical called psilocybin which can cause hallucinations. Magic mushrooms are eaten fresh, dried, or crushed and mixed with food. The trip from mushrooms can be similar to the trip from LSD, and it cannot be predicted. The hallucinations can last for six to ten hours and can be frightening. Users have reported seeing heads popping out of walls and imaginary bugs crawling on their bodies.

CHAPTER 5

Stimulants

Stimulants are drugs that speed up the functions of the body: the heart beats faster and blood pressure rises.

People high on stimulants experience feelings of false euphoria, or happiness, that can last from thirty seconds to two hours. Although stimulants may give users energy and make them feel alert, they soon become nervous and unfocused. Stimulants are highly addictive drugs.

Long-term effects of stimulant use include damage to the mind and body and can eventually lead to death.

Drugs in this category include amphetamines, cocaine or crack cocaine, methamphetamine, Ecstasy, and crank.

Amphetamines

Amphetamines are synthetic drugs that usually come in pill, capsule, and tablet form. They are usually swallowed, but they can also be dissolved and injected under the skin or crushed and "snorted" through the nose.

Amphetamines make the user feel alert and full of pep. Over time, however, users may become hyperactive and restless. They may become angry easily, or violent. They may also become paranoid, or fear that everyone is turning against them.

When the drug wears off, most users fall into a deep depression. Some have attempted suicide rather than face this depression.

Withdrawal from amphetamines is long and difficult and must be done under the supervision of a doctor.

Cocaine

Cocaine is made from the leaves of the coca plant. Cocaine is a white powder. Because the pure form of cocaine is so powerful, it is usually cut, or mixed, with other substances before it hits the streets. These include baking soda, talcum powder, or rat poison.

Cocaine can be taken into the body in different ways. In powder form, it can be snorted through the nose. In liquid form, it can be

Cocaine users make elaborate preparations to snort a line of cocaine.

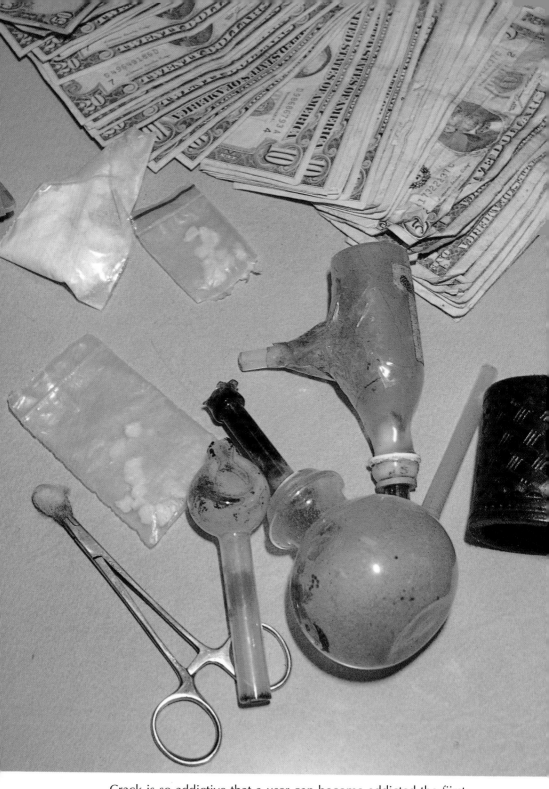

Crack is so addictive that a user can become addicted the fiirst time he or she uses it.

injected into the bloodstream. This is called mainlining. Treated with a chemical called petroleum ether, powdered cocaine forms a paste. When this paste is heated, the vapors can be inhaled. This is called freebasing. Freebasing is very dangerous. The vapors are much stronger than cocaine in powder form. Also, when the chemicals are heated, they become unstable and can explode. The user can be burned or killed.

Cocaine gives users a rush of energy. They feel self confident, happy, and able to do anything. This high lasts for about half an hour. When the drug wears off, the user crashes and goes into a deep depression. He or she may feel confused, angry, anxious, or sad. Most users cannot stand these feelings and will turn to cocaine to lift them up again. This often becomes a never-ending cycle.

Users always face the danger of overdosing on cocaine. Because cocaine isn't regulated, users never know how pure their cocaine is. If they use a hit of cocaine that is purer than they are used to, they may overdose and die.

Crack

Crack is a pure form of cocaine, and it is extremely addictive. A person can become addicted the first time he or she uses it.

Crack is made by mixing cocaine with

40 baking powder and water and boiling the mixture into a paste. When it hardens, it forms a "rock" that can be smoked.

A high from crack lasts five to seven minutes and ends with a crash that is worse than that of cocaine. The pain and depression from the crash is so bad that most people will do anything to get high again.

The lure of crack is its seemingly cheap price. But the highs are so short that users need to smoke crack several times to maintain a high. This habit can become costly fast.

Both crack and cocaine cause increases in blood pressure, body temperature, and breathing rate. These drugs can kill even first-time users. They often also cause violent and erratic behavior.

Methamphetamine

Methamphetamine is a synthetic drug and is dangerous for both users and the people who make it. It also known as crank or ice.

The high from methamphetamine is almost immediate and lasts for two to six hours. It is snorted or injected into a vein. The high is intense, but it also often leaves users paranoid and prone to violent behavior.

Methamphetamine is usually made by untrained people in makeshift labs in

Pushers hang around schoolyards hoping to snare new customers at an early age.

people's basements, bathrooms, or kitchens. Because the people are untrained and the conditions so unsanitary, the drug is often poorly made. Users have become sick or died from poorly made methamphetamine.

The chemicals necessary to make methamphetamine are so unstable that many makers of the drug have died when their illegal meth labs exploded.

Over time, this drug can cause brain damage and psychotic behavior.

CHAPTER 6

Narcotics

*M*ost narcotics are opiates, which means the drugs are made from the poppy plant. There are, however, synthetic versions of narcotics which act similarly to the natural versions. Throughout history opiates have been used to treat ailments, such as cramps, headaches, strokes, and depression. But when people realized the how addictive the drugs were, regulations were established to control their use.

Today narcotics can only be prescribed by doctors for medical purposes. They are used to help patients suffering from chronic pain. They can also be used on patients to ease pain after surgery.

Narcotics are similar to depressants in

that they slow down the functions of the | *43*
body. But unlike depressants, narcotics
relieve pain. Drugs in this category include
heroin, morphine, and methadone.

Heroin

Heroin is one of the most addictive and
widely-used narcotics. Heroin is also called
"Big H," "Horse," or "Smack."

According to the 1995 National Household Survey on Drug Abuse, 1.4 million
people in the United States have used
heroin. Usually a white or brown powder,
heroin can be swallowed, smoked, or snorted, but the method used to achieve the
most intense high is injecting it into a vein.

Heroin reaches the brain in a matter of
seconds. The user experiences a burst of
euphoria for a few minutes. Then he or she
feels a less intense high for four or five
hours. This is often followed by nausea,
vomiting, watery eyes, and drowsiness.

It is easy to overdose on heroin, especially if it is mixed with other drugs, such
as alcohol. This combination can lead to
convulsions, coma, and even death. According to the New York State Office of Alcoholism and Substance Abuse, there is a link
between smoking heroin and an incurable
neurological condition that affects muscle

Junkies spend most of their time shooting up—or thinking about it.

coordination and speech.

Users who inject heroin also face the danger of contracting diseases from dirty needles, such as hepatitis and HIV.

Because heroin is highly addictive, it is illegal in the United States.

China White

China White is a synthetic version of heroin. China White is more potent than heroin. It is extremely addictive and dangerous. Like heroin, China White comes in the form of a white powder and can be smoked, snorted, or injected.

Because China White is more potent than heroin, it is very easy to overdose on it. Many users who believe they are using heroin are in fact using China White. Believing that it is heroin, users may take their usual dose, and overdose on the China White.

Side effects of using China White include constipation, uncontrollable shaking, and slowed breathing and heart rate.

Morphine

Morphine is a weaker narcotic than heroin, but it is also very addictive. Morphine can legally be prescribed by doctors for patients in chronic pain. It is effective in treating the pain of cancer patients. However, most

46 doctors are reluctant to prescribe it because of the addictive nature of the drug.

Morphine usually comes in the form of white crystals or powder. It was first used during the American Civil War by doctors to treat wounded soldiers. Even as late as 1900, morphine was an ingredient in medicines for the treatment of various ailments. Once people realized how addictive it was, laws were created to restrict its use.

Methadone

Methadone is a synthetic drug used to treat heroin addiction. When dosages are properly prescribed by a doctor, they keep heroin addicts from suffering withdrawal symptoms without getting high. But methadone is also addictive. Methadone is only legal when it is prescribed by doctors and used for the purpose of ending heroin addiction.

Methadone comes in the form of pills, tablets, or liquid. Unlike heroin, methadone has a slower onset. The drug is stored in the liver, and is released slowly. Patients only need to take one dose of methadone each day.

Patients can be maintained on methadone for years. Patients who want to quit using methadone are weaned off the drug so they do not suffer any withdrawal symptoms which may cause them to use heroin again. | *47*

Heroin addicts who want to go on methadone must be accepted by a methadone clinic and be willing to participate in therapy. Most methadone clinics first stabilize their patients on methadone so their bodies don't crave heroin. They also offer therapy with trained counselors to try to solve whatever problems led the addict to use heroin.

Some patients, however, sneak methadone out of the clinics and sell it illegally on the streets. Heroin addicts who cannot afford to buy heroin may buy methadone illegally so they don't have to suffer from withdrawal symptoms.

CHAPTER 7

Depressants

*D*epressants are a class of drugs that slow down the functions of the body, including mental alertness, heart rate, and reflex time. These drugs are often referred to as "downers." According to a recent study by the National Institute for Drugs and Alcohol, about 6 percent of seniors in high school have used depressants.

Drugs in this category include anti-anxiety and antipsychotic medications, sleeping pills, barbiturates, sedatives, and muscle relaxants. These drugs are legally prescribed by doctors for medical conditions, but they are often illegally sold on the streets. Goofballs, barbs, blue devils, yellow jackets, and ludes are some of the names for these drugs on the streets.

Depressants change the chemistry in the **49** brain. They can cause confusion, slurred speech, and loss of coordination. Larger doses are dangerous and can lead to respiratory failure, coma, and possibly death. Depressants can also be addictive when used over a period of time.

Barbiturates

There over 2,500 different kinds of barbiturates. Each barbiturate is made for a specific ailment. They come in pills or capsules, and are either swallowed or dissolved in liquid and injected into a vein.

Barbiturates are used as sedatives to relax the central nervous system. They are often used before surgery to put a patient to sleep. They are also used to control health conditions, such as high blood pressure, epilepsy, and ulcers.

A person on barbiturates may become confused, slur his words, and stagger or lose his balance. Barbiturate users often appear drunk.

Barbiturates are addictive. It only takes one to two months of taking doses higher than the amount recommended by a doctor for someone to grow dependent on them. Barbiturates should only be used under the supervision of a doctor.

50 | *Tranquilizers*

Addiction to tranquilizers is one of the most common drug-abuse problems in the United States. It is this addiction that leads many people to enter drug rehabilitation centers every year.

Although doctors can legally prescribe tranquilizers for their patients, they are very addictive drugs. Even people who follow their doctors orders and take the recommended dosages can become dependent on them.

Some of the most commonly prescribed tranquilizers—Valium, Xanax, and Librium—all belong to a group of drugs called benzodiazepines. Doctors often prescribe them to treat tension resulting from day-to-day stress. Patients who are on these drugs for too long or use too high a dosage risk the possibility of becoming addicted. Even people who take low dosages over a prolonged period of time risk becoming addicted.

Withdrawal symptoms include anxiety, restlessness, nausea, loss of appetite, tremors, sleeping problems, and muscle pain. In severe cases, a person may have convulsions.

CHAPTER 8

Living a Drug-Free Life

*I*t was Kim's first day of school since she was released from the drug rehab center. She was a little nervous because she thought everyone at school must know that she was in drug rehab. Kim had been in rehab for a month trying to kick her cocaine habit. It wasn't easy, but she did it. She was determined never to let drugs get in her way again.

She was walking to homeroom when she heard her name. She turned and saw Sherry coming toward her. Sherry said welcome back and asked Kim if she wanted to come to a party tonight at her place. Sherry was the one who had introduced Kim to cocaine during one of her parties.

When Kim didn't say anything, Sherry said, "Come on, it'll be fun. It must have been

Teens who don't use drugs are better able to accomplish their goals in life.

tough for you in rehab. You haven't had a hit for over a month. How can you stand it? I've got a stash of some really good coke."

Kim felt her stomach tighten as she thought about how good the rush from the coke would make her feel. But then she remembered how bad she felt when she came down from her high. She remembered the tears in her mom's eyes this morning when she told Kim how proud she was of her, that she was strong enough to overcome her addiction.

Kim tightened her hands into fists. "Look Sherry, I don't think that's a good idea. Coke just isn't my thing anymore. I'll see you around," said Kim as she turned and walked away from Sherry.

Kim knew she had taken her first step to living a life free from drugs. She was ready to deal with her problems without help from a drug.

It takes strength and courage to live a drug-free life. This is true for recovering addicts and for people who have never tried drugs but have been tempted. Everyone faces problems and stress at some point. Sometimes it may seem like a great idea to take some drug and escape from your problems. But think carefully before getting involved with drugs. Life is full of choices. You have to think about all the pros and cons involved in your decisions and make

54 the right choice for yourself. Don't let anyone pressure you to do something you're not comfortable with.

Peer Pressure

Friends may pressure you to try drugs. Although some teens know it is wrong and dangerous to try drugs, they follow their friends because they don't want to be left out or be thought of as a geek for not going along with everyone else. Peer pressure is one of the biggest influences for teens to experiment with drugs. Keep in mind, however, that true friends will respect and support whatever decision you make.

Another method you can use to avoid this pressure is to never put yourself in a situation where drugs are involved. If you are invited to a party where you know drugs will become an issue, don't go. Instead hang out with other friends who share the same opinions about drugs.

Influences of Family Members

There are teens whose drug habits may have resulted from influences in the home. They may see siblings abusing drugs or parents popping pills or drinking alcohol. If other family members are abusing drugs, teens may have easy access to these drugs.

Peer pressure is one of the biggest influences on teens to experiment with drugs.

56 Teens who see family members using drugs may think that using drugs is normal or acceptable. They may be curious and can easily steal drugs from medicine cabinets or wherever the drugs are kept.

Coping with Stress

Many people use drugs as an escape from the stress of everyday life. But stress is a normal part of life. It often makes us work harder and strive for more. Drugs may temporarily relieve stress, but the stress will still be there once the high from the drug wears off. Instead of trying to escape from stress, learn to deal with it.

How do you cope with the stress in your life? Involve yourself in a project that makes you feel good. Start an exercise program, join a school club, or write your feelings out in a journal.

As we have discussed in this book, when drugs become a problem in a neighborhood, other problems, such as gangs and violence, will also develop. But the only way for drugs to enter a neighborhood is if there is a market. Inform others about the dangers of drugs. By saying no to drugs you are helping to keep yourself and your neighborhood safe.

Glossary

addict Person who cannot control his or her use of drugs.

amphetamine Drug that stimulates the central nervous system.

barbiturate Drug that depresses the central nervous system.

dopamine A chemical found in the brain that may be responsible for addiction.

drug Substance that changes the way a person's body works.

drug abuse Intentional taking of a substance to change the way a person feels or behaves.

drug-dependence Reliance on a drug as a method of escaping prolems or dealing with life issues.

58 | **illegal drug** Drug not permitted by law for sale or use.

legal drug Drug allowed to be sold by law.

natural drug Drug obtained from plants.

prescription drug Drug prescribed as medication by a doctor.

psychoactive drug Drug that changes a person's behavior.

schizophrenia Psychotic disorder characterized by hallucinations or paranoia.

synthetic drug Drug made from chemicals; not natural.

Where to Go For Help

American Council for Drug Education
204 Monroe Street
Rockville, MD 20850
(301) 294-0600

Narcotics Anonymous
P.O. Box 9999
Van Nuys, CA 94109
(818) 773-9999

National Clearinghouse for Alcohol and
   Drug Information
P.O. Box 2345
Rockville, MD 20852
(800) 729-6686
Web site: http://www.health.org

60 | National Council on Alcoholism & Drug
Dependence
12 West 21st Street
New York, NY 10010
(800) 622-2255

In Canada
Alcohol and Drug Dependency Information
and Counseling Services
2471 1/2 Portage Avenue, #2
Winnipeg, MB R3J 0N6
(204) 831-1999

For Further Reading

Ball, Jacqueline. *Everything You Need to Know About Drug Abuse*, rev. ed. New York: Rosen Publishing Group, 1998.

Edwards, Gabrielle. *Coping with Drug Abuse*, rev. ed. New York: Rosen Publishing Group, 1990.

Godfrey, Martin. *Heroin*. New York: Franklin Watts, 1987.

Kaplan, Leslie. *Coping with Peer Pressure*, rev. ed. New York: Rosen Publishing Group, 1993.

Lee, Essie E. *Breaking the Connection*. New York: Julian Messner, 1988.

McFarland, Rhoda. *Coping with Substance Abuse*, rev. ed. New York: Rosen Publishing Group, 1990.

Smith, Sandra Lee. *Coping with Decision-*

62 *Making*, rev. ed. New York: Rosen
Publishing Group, 1994.

Smith, Sandra Lee. *Value of Self-Control.*
New York: Rosen Publishing Group,
1994.

Sunshine, Linda and John Wright. *The
Best Treatment Centers for Alcoholism and
Drug Abuse.* New York: Avon Books,
1988.

Index

64

About the Author

Mrs. Gabrielle I. Edwards was Assistant Principal Supervision of the Science Department at Franklin D. Roosevelt High School in Brooklyn, New York. She supervised science instruction for 3,200 young people.

Mrs. Edwards is the author of several books for students in junior and senior high school, including *Coping with Drug Abuse, Biology the Easy Way,* and *Living Things* (co-authored).

Photo Credits

Cover photo by Chris Volpe; p. 2 © Frank Fisher/Gamma-Liaison; pp. 8, 12, 16, 21, 24, 33, 37, 41, 52 by Chris Volpe; p. 29 by Lauren Piperno; p. 38 © John Chiasson/Gamma-Liaison; p. 44 by Chuck Peterson/Blackbirch Graphics; p. 55 by Stuart Rabinowitz.